MY FIRST SPORTS
Tennis

by Anne Wendorff

BLASTOFF! READERS 4

BELLWETHER MEDIA • MINNEAPOLIS, MN

Note to Librarians, Teachers, and Parents:

Blastoff! Readers are carefully developed by literacy experts and combine standards-based content with developmentally appropriate text.

Level 1 provides the most support through repetition of high-frequency words, light text, predictable sentence patterns, and strong visual support.

Level 2 offers early readers a bit more challenge through varied simple sentences, increased text load, and less repetition of high-frequency words.

Level 3 advances early-fluent readers toward fluency through increased text and concept load, less reliance on visuals, longer sentences, and more literary language.

Level 4 builds reading stamina by providing more text per page, increased use of punctuation, greater variation in sentence patterns, and increasingly challenging vocabulary.

Level 5 encourages children to move from "learning to read" to "reading to learn" by providing even more text, varied writing styles, and less familiar topics.

Whichever book is right for your reader, Blastoff! Readers are the perfect books to build confidence and encourage a love of reading that will last a lifetime!

This edition first published in 2010 by Bellwether Media, Inc.

No part of this publication may be reproduced in whole or in part without written permission of the publisher. For information regarding permission, write to Bellwether Media, Inc., Attention: Permissions Department, Post Office Box 19349, Minneapolis, MN 55419.

Library of Congress Cataloging-in-Publication Data
Wendorff, Anne.
  Tennis / by Anne Wendorff.
    p. cm. – (Blastoff! readers. My first sports)
  Includes bibliographical references and index.
  Summary: "Simple text and full color photographs introduce beginning readers to the sport of tennis. Developed by literacy experts for students in grades two through five"–Provided by publisher.
  ISBN 978-1-60014-328-1 (hardcover : alk. paper)
  1. Tennis–Juvenile literature. I. Title.
GV996.5.W46 2009
796.342–dc22

2009008188

Text copyright © 2010 by Bellwether Media, Inc. BLASTOFF! READERS and associated logos are trademarks and/or registered trademarks of Bellwether Media, Inc. Printed in the United States of America.

SCHOLASTIC, CHILDREN'S PRESS, and associated logos are trademarks and/or registered trademarks of Scholastic Inc.

Contents

What Is Tennis?	4
The Basic Rules of Tennis	8
Tennis Equipment	18
Tennis Today	20
Glossary	22
To Learn More	23
Index	24

What Is Tennis?

Tennis is a sport played by two or four people. A player uses a **racket** to hit a tennis ball over a net to an opponent. Players try to make their opponents miss the ball.

Modern tennis was invented in England. In the 1800s, an Englishman named Walter Clopton Wingfield created a sport based on an old game played by French royalty.

He called the sport "lawn tennis." In lawn tennis, players hit a ball over a net with a racket. Modern tennis is based on the rules of lawn tennis.

The Basic Rules of Tennis

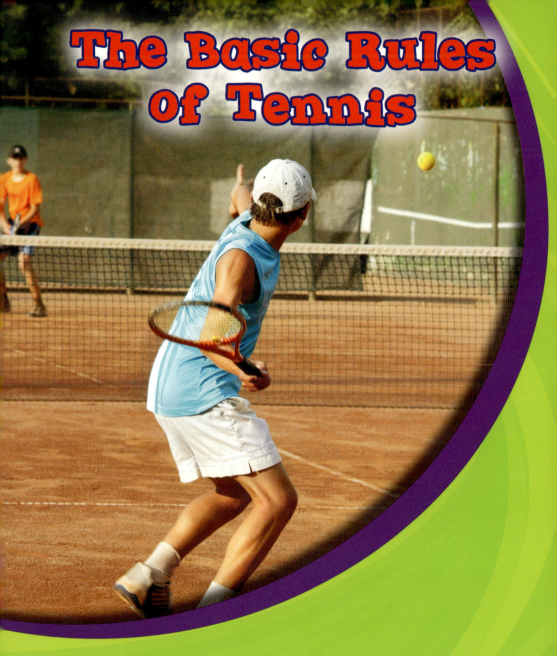

In tennis, players hit a ball back and forth over a net. Players score points when their opponents hit the ball out-of-bounds or do not hit the ball over the net.

When two people play each other, it is called singles tennis. When two teams of two people play each other, it is called doubles tennis.

A tennis **match** is made up of three to five **sets**. A set is made up of six or more **games**. To win a set, players need to win six games and lead their opponents by two.

Players need to win more sets than their opponents to win a match. A **tiebreak game** is played if the score of a set is tied.

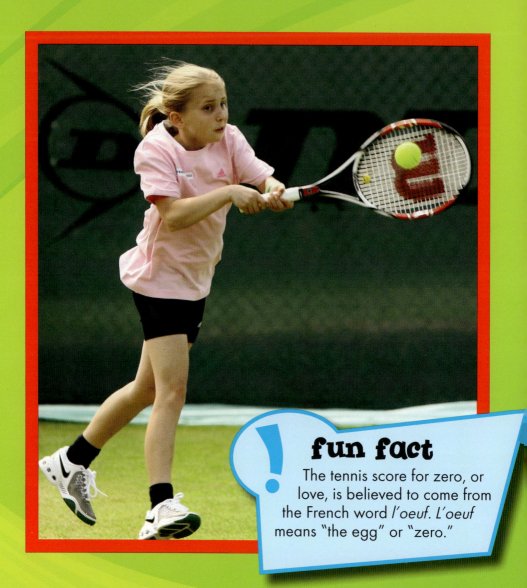

fun fact
The tennis score for zero, or love, is believed to come from the French word *l'oeuf*. *L'oeuf* means "the egg" or "zero."

Each game involves scoring four points. Every point has a name. Having zero points is called "love." Having one point is called "15." Having two points is called "30." Having three points is called "40."

A game is over when a player scores four points and leads by two. If both players have a score of 40, it is called **deuce**. A player must win two points back-to-back from deuce to win the game.

fun fact
Most tennis courts are made of clay, cement, or grass.

Tennis matches are played on **courts**. Tennis courts are 78 feet (24 meters) long and 36 feet (11 meters) wide. A net divides the court. The net is 3.5 feet (1.1 meters) high.

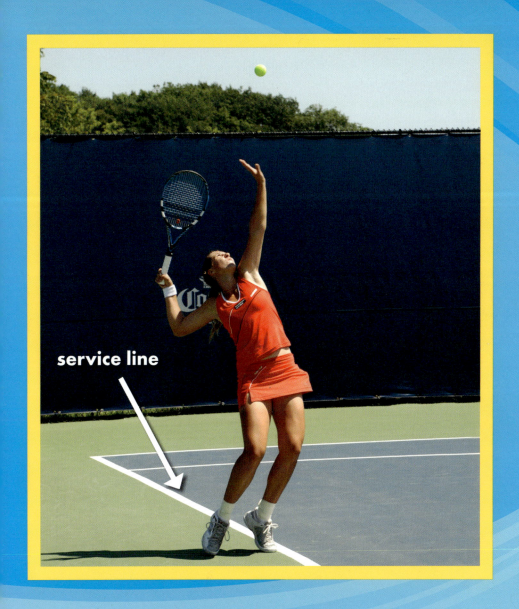

service line

The **service line** is a white line at the end of each half of the court. Players must **serve** the ball from the service line. Players serve by throwing the ball into the air and hitting it over the net.

forehand shot

There are many ways to hit the ball after the serve. The most common ways to hit the ball are called a **forehand shot** and a **backhand shot**.

Players also use **lob shots** to hit the ball over their opponents' heads and **drop shots** to land the ball just over the net. They can also smash the ball into the ground with powerful **overhead slams**.

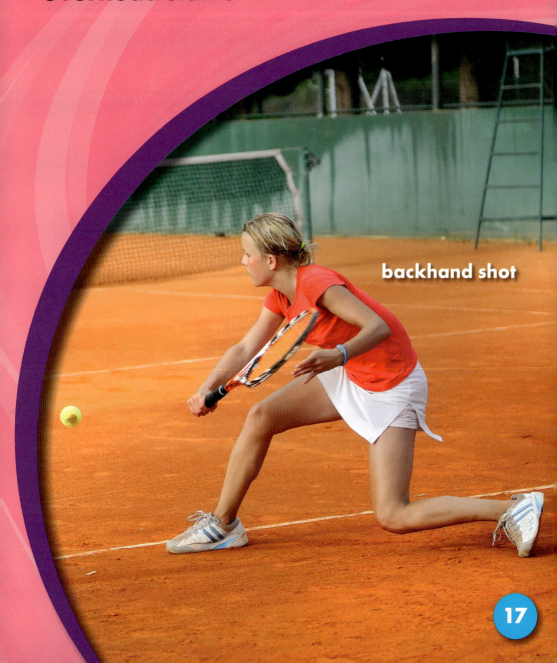

backhand shot

Tennis Equipment

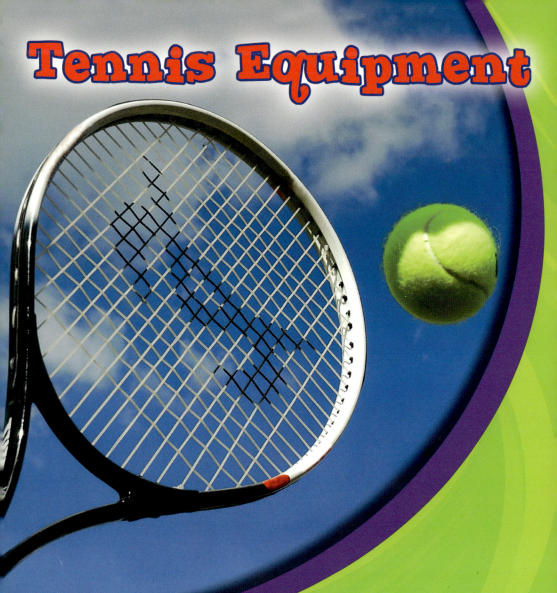

A racket and a ball are the main pieces of equipment in tennis. Players wear tennis shoes to grip the ground while they run on the court.

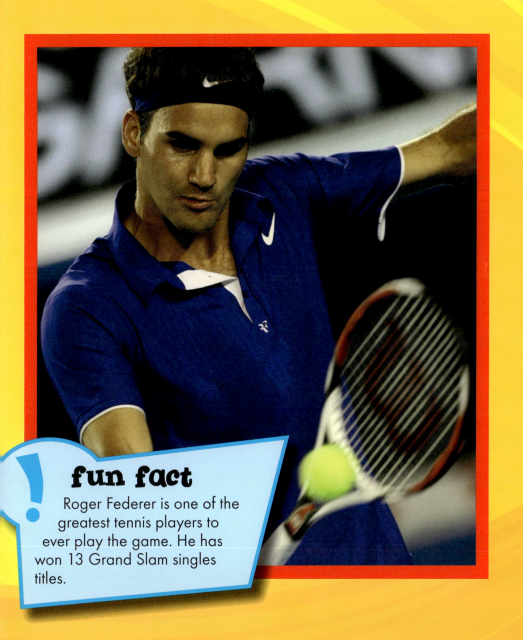

fun fact
Roger Federer is one of the greatest tennis players to ever play the game. He has won 13 Grand Slam singles titles.

Some players wear sweatbands on their heads and wrists to keep sweat away from their eyes and hands.

Tennis Today

Rafael Nadal

Professional tennis players compete in tournaments. The four biggest tournaments are called **Grand Slam** tournaments.

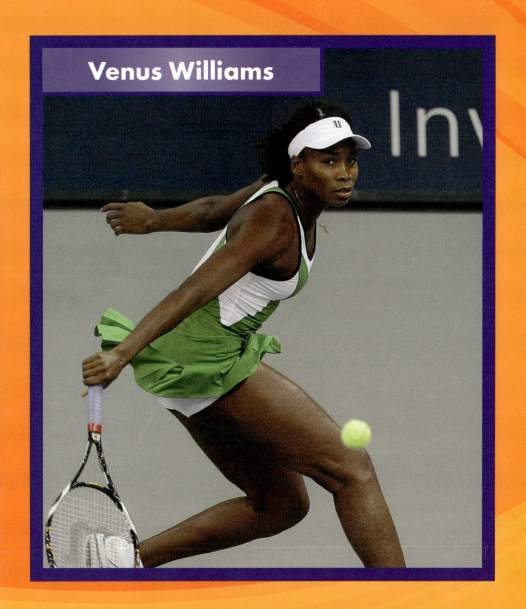
Venus Williams

Tennis fans pack stadiums to watch players such as Roger Federer, Rafael Nadal, and Venus and Serena Williams. The two best players in each tournament compete in an exciting final match to determine the winner.

Glossary

backhand shot—a ball hit with the back of the player's hand facing forward

court—the area where a tennis match is played

deuce—a tied score at 40; a player must win two points back-to-back to win the game.

drop shot—a ball that is hit so that it barely passes over the net

forehand shot—a ball hit with the player's palm facing forward

game—a part of a set where two players or teams play to four points; one player or team needs to win six games to win one set.

Grand Slam—the four major professional tournaments; they are the U.S. Open, the French Open, the Australian Open, and Wimbledon.

lob shot—a ball that is hit over an opponent's head

match—three to five sets of tennis

overhead slam—a powerful hit that slams the ball over the net and into the ground

racket—a piece of tennis equipment that is used to hit the ball over the net

serve—when a player hits the ball to begin a point; one player serves the ball to the other.

service line—a white line that players must stand behind while they serve

set—a part of a tennis match made up of at least six games; the winner of a set must win by two games.

tiebreak game—a game of tennis that is played when a set is tied; tiebreak games are played to seven points; one player or team must win by two points.

To Learn More

AT THE LIBRARY
Ditchfield, Christin. *Tennis*. New York, N.Y.: Children's Press, 2003.

Marsico, Katie and Cecilia Minden. *Tennis*. Mankato, Minn.: Cherry Lake, 2009.

Wells, Don. *For the Love of Tennis*. New York, N.Y.: Weigl, 2005.

ON THE WEB
Learning more about tennis is as easy as 1, 2, 3.

1. Go to www.factsurfer.com.

2. Enter "tennis" into the search box.

3. Click the "Surf" button and you will see a list of related Web sites.

With factsurfer.com, finding more information is just a click away.

Index

backhand shot, 16, 17
courts, 14, 15, 18
deuce, 13
doubles tennis, 9
drop shots, 17
England, 6
equipment, 18
Federer, Roger, 19, 21
forehand shot, 16
games, 10, 12, 13, 19
Grand Slam, 19, 20
lawn tennis, 7
lob shots, 17
match, 10, 11, 14, 21
Nadal, Rafael, 20, 21
net, 4, 7, 8, 14, 15, 17
overhead slams, 17
points, 8, 12, 13
racket, 4, 7, 18
serve, 15, 16
service line, 15
sets, 10, 11
singles tennis, 9
sweatbands, 19
tennis shoes, 18

tiebreak game, 11
tournaments, 20, 21
Williams, Serena, 21
Williams, Venus, 21
Wingfield, Walter Clopton, 6

The images in this book are reproduced through the courtesy of: Peter Weber, front cover, p. 13; Alvis Upitis, pp. 4-5; Quinn Rooney / Getty Images, p. 6; Mary Evans Picture Library / The Image Works, p. 7; Serghei Starus, p. 8; Cameron Spencer / Getty Images, p. 9; Lori Adamski Peek / Getty Images, p. 10; Joe McDaniel, p. 11; Matthew Lewis / Stringer / Getty Images, pp. 12, 16; Clive Brunskill / Getty Images, p. 14; ulga, p. 15; Benis Arapovic, p. 17; Stephen Rudolph, p. 18; Greg Wood / Getty Images, p. 19; Hamish Blair / Getty Images, p. 20; Thomas Niedermueller / Getty Images, p. 21.